Dehydrating Food:
Simple and Easy Dehydrator Recipes

Cathy L. Kidd

Table of Contents

Introduction

This next book in my series of recipe books is for your Dehydrator. Over time, I've developed a specialty of providing what you want most – the Recipes! That's why I call them recipe books not cookbooks. I don't include all the information and fluff you already know – just great recipes you can try as is or modify to your tastes. I do include any special instructions you'll need to know for some of the recipes.

All of the recipes in my books work well with modification of the ingredients. There are some variations listed with some of them but feel free to be creative and try something new!

The recipes in this book fall into two categories. Recipes for dehydrating and recipes for items and meals that use dehydrated ingredients. The manual that came with your dehydrator will give you instructions on how to use it and basic guidelines on how to prepare foods for dehydrating and how long they will take to dry. In the Index for this book, I've listed the recipes by category for you.

90% of the manuals say it takes some experimentation to get the best results. In my experience everything came out great the first time! The only exception is fruit rolls and leathers. If you make them too thin they will fall apart and you'll just have crumbs. So don't be stingy when you make them! If you do get crumbs, then just use them as a topping on ice cream, salads or cottage cheese. No need to let anything go to waste.

A number of the recipes call for fruit roll or mesh sheets. If you don't have them, you can line the trays with plastic wrap being sure not to cover the center hole or the side vent holes. You can also do a smaller version of the recipe and put it on the bottom tray with other things on the racks above.

So make something great today and visit my Facebook page to tell us about it:
Recipes For Your Kitchen Appliances
https://www.facebook.com/RecipesForYourKitchenAppliances

Note: The photos in this book are in black and white to save publishing cost and keep the price low for you. If you'd like to see the color versions please visit us at
http://books.easyhomemadebreadrecipes.com/dehydratorphotos

The Recipes

Fruit Rolls/Leathers

To make your fruit rolls and leathers, mix all of the ingredients in a blender or food processor until smooth. Pour the mixture onto fruit roll sheets placed on the racks of your dehydrator. Experiment with spraying a little olive oil on the sheets first so your fruit leather won't stick when dried.

When pouring the mixture, don't be stingy! If you make it too thin, you won't get good, solid rolls. About 1/4" thick should be perfect.

Dry for 4-8 hours or until leathery and pliable but not sticky. Remove from the sheets while warm and let them cool a little. Roll in plastic wrap and store in a cool, dry place like your refrigerator or freezer.

To rehydrate any of the leathers, add 1 cup of water to each cup of leather and let sit until it reaches the consistency you want.

The leather pictured here is Applesauce and Strawberry with banana chips on top.

Apple and Cheese

4	Apples, peeled, cored and chopped
1/2 cup	Cheddar cheese, grated
1/2 teaspoon	Cinnamon
1/2 teaspoon	Nutmeg
3/4 cup	Pecans, ground

Note: The pecans can be added to the blender with the other ingredients or sprinkled on top of the leather before drying.

Apple and Orange

1 1/2 cups	Applesauce
1 small	Apple, peeled, cored and chopped
2 teaspoons	Dried orange, ground
1-1/2 teaspoons	Vanilla

Apple and Yogurt

6	Apples, peeled, cored and chopped
1/2 teaspoon	Cinnamon
1/4 teaspoon	Cloves
1 cup	Plain non-fat yogurt, any flavor
2 1/2 teaspoons	Nutmeg

Applesauce

2 pounds	Apples, peeled, cored and chopped
1/2 cup	Water
1/4 cup	Lemon juice
1/2 cup	Sugar
1 teaspoon	Cinnamon

Simmer the apples in a saucepan with the water until softened. Put the lemon juice in a blender and gradually add the apples, mixing until puréed. Add the sugar and cinnamon and mix well. Pour the mixture on a fruit roll sheet and dry.

Note: For a quick and easy version, use one 24 ounce jar of applesauce, any flavor. Depending on the type of applesauce you use, you may want to reduce the sugar.

Applesauce and Strawberry

3 cups	Applesauce, prepared or homemade
3 cups	Strawberries, sliced

Applesauce and Banana

2 cups	Applesauce, prepared or homemade
2 cups	Bananas, cut into pieces

Banana and Orange

6	Bananas, peeled and cut into pieces
1	Orange, peeled and quartered

Boysenberry

1 quart	Boysenberries

After blending them, strain them through cheesecloth to remove the seeds.

Cantaloupe

1 cup	Cantaloupe, diced
1/3 cup	Applesauce
2 tablespoons	Coconut flakes
3 tablespoons	Slivered almonds
Dash	Cinnamon

Note: The almonds and cinnamon can be added to the blender with the other ingredients or sprinkled on top of the leather before drying.

Cherry and Rhubarb

| 1 (21 oz.) can | Cherry pie filling |
| 1 cup | Raw rhubarb, diced |

Simmer the cherry pie filling and rhubarb in saucepan for about 10 minutes until rhubarb is tender. Cool. Purée the mixture in a blender and pour onto fruit leather sheets.

Note: As a variation try strawberry pie filling in place of the cherry.

Peanut Butter and Yogurt

1 (8 oz.) container	Banana or vanilla yogurt
2	Bananas, cut into pieces
1/4 cup	Peanuts
2 tablespoons	Honey

Pineapple and Coconut

| 1 (20 oz.) can | Unsweetened pineapple chunks or rings |
| 1 cup | Coconut |

Raspberry and Chocolate

1/2 cup	Frozen raspberries, thawed and drained
1/2 cup	Dark or white chocolate bits, melted
1/3 cup	White grape juice
1/2 cup	Applesauce, flavored

Strawberry and Cream Cheese

1 quart	Strawberries, washed and cored
1/2 cup	Slivered toasted almonds
1 (8 oz.) package	Cream Cheese

Strawberry Daiquiri

1 quart	Strawberries, washed and cored
1/2	Lime, peeled and quartered
2 teaspoons	Honey
1/8 teaspoon	Rum extract

Strawberry Rhubarb

1 cup	Rhubarb
1/4 cup	Water
2 cups	Strawberries
1/2 cup	Honey

Simmer the rhubarb and water in a saucepan for approximately 5 minutes until the rhubarb is tender. Cool, drain and add the rhubarb to the rest of the ingredients in a blender.

Yogurt

Yogurt, any flavor

Experiment until you find the brand which dries most evenly and gives you the best flavor.

Baked Goods/Breakfast

Apricot Jam

1 1/2 cups	Dried apricots, coarsely diced
1 cup	Water
3/4 cup	Honey
1 teaspoon	Grated lemon peel
	—or—
1/2 teaspoon	Dried lemon peel, powdered
1/2 cup	Walnuts or pecans, chopped (optional)

Bring the apricots and water to a boil in a small saucepan. Remove from the heat, cover, and let stand 30 minutes.

Add the honey and lemon peel and bring it to a second boil. Boil gently, uncovered, over medium heat for 10 minutes or until the jam is the consistency you want. Stir in the nuts if desired. Pour into jars and seal.

Note: Almost any fruit or berry can be substituted for the apricots. Try peach for a really good version.

Apricot Coffee Cake

2 1⁄4 cups	All purpose flour
3⁄4 cup	Brown sugar
3⁄4 cup	Butter
1⁄2 teaspoon	Baking powder
1⁄2 teaspoon	Baking soda
1⁄4 teaspoon	Salt
3⁄4 cup	Sour cream
2	Eggs
1 teaspoon	Almond extract
8 ounces	Cream cheese
1⁄4 cup	White sugar
1⁄2 cup	Apricot preserves
1 cup	Dried apricots, chopped
1⁄2 cup	Slivered almonds

Preheat your oven to 350°F. Grease and flour a 10 inch spring form pan. Combine the flour and brown sugar and cut in the butter until the mixture is crumbly. Set aside 1 cup of the crumb mixture.

Add the baking powder, baking soda, salt, sour cream, 1 egg, and almond extract to the remaining crumb mixture. Blend well. Spread the batter over the bottom and the sides of the pan.

Combine the cream cheese, white sugar, and remaining egg. Pour the mixture over the batter in the pan. Carefully add the preserves and finely chopped dried apricots on top of the cream cheese mixture.

Combine the set aside crumb mixture and slivered almonds and sprinkle over top.

Bake for 45 to 50 minutes or until the cream cheese filling is set and the crust is a deep golden brown.
Cool for 15 minutes before removing the sides of the pan. It can be served warm or cool.

Apricot Muffins

1/2 cup	Margarine
1/2 cup	Sugar
2	Eggs
1 cup	Milk
1	Orange, juice and grated rind
1 1/2 cups	Flour
3/4 cup	Dried apricots, chopped

Preheat your oven to 350°F. Grease the bottoms of twelve muffin tins or use muffin liners.

Combine the margarine and sugar with an electric beater. Beat in the eggs, milk and orange juice.

Fold in the flour, apricots and orange rind and spoon into prepared muffin tins.

Bake for 25 minutes or until a wooden toothpick inserted in center comes out clean.

Banana Bread (Version 1)

3/4 cup	Margarine or butter
1 1/2 cups	Sugar
2	Eggs
1 teaspoon	Vanilla
1 1/2 cups	Ripe banana, mashed
2 cups	Flour
1 teaspoon	Soda
1/2 teaspoon	Salt
1/2 cup	Buttermilk
1/2 cup	Dried banana, chopped
1/2 cup	Dates, chopped
1/2 cup	Pecans, chopped
2 tablespoons	Raw sugar

Preheat your oven to 350°F. Grease and flour 3 small (3" x 5") or two medium (3-1/2" x 7-1/2") loaf pans.

Combine the margarine or butter and sugar and mix well. Add the eggs and vanilla. Add the mashed banana.

Combine the flour, soda, and salt and mix well. Add the flour mixture to the margarine mixture alternating with the buttermilk, until they blend well.

Fold in the dried banana, pecans, and dates. Pour into prepared pans. Sprinkle raw sugar over tops of loaves.

Bake for 45 minutes, until a wooden toothpick inserted in center comes out clean. Cool 10 minutes in the pan before removing.

Note: You can add dried pineapple instead of dates for a different taste.

Banana Bread (Version 2)

1 cup	Dried bananas, powdered
1 1/2 cups	Milk
1/2 cup	Margarine
1 cup	Sugar
2	Eggs
2 cups	Flour, whole wheat and/or white
1 1/2 teaspoons	Baking powder
1/2 teaspoon	Baking soda
1/4 teaspoon	Salt
1/2 cup	Nuts, chopped

Preheat your oven to 350°F. Grease and flour 1-2 loaf pans.

Combine the bananas and milk and let it sit for 10 minutes to rehydrate the bananas. Combine the margarine and sugar. Add the eggs and beat.

Combine the flour, baking powder, baking soda and salt and mix well. Combine the rehydrated bananas and flour mixture alternating a half cup or so at a time. Beat the mixture after each addition. Stir in the nuts.

Pour into the loaf pan(s) and let the batter sit for 10 minutes before baking.

Bake 50-60 minutes or until toothpick inserted in the center comes out clean. Cool before removing from pan.

Banana Bread (Version 3)

1 1/2 cups	Dried banana pieces
2 cups	Water
3/4 cup	Butter or margarine
1 1/2 cups	Brown sugar
2	Eggs
3/4 cup	Milk
1/2 cup	Crunchy peanut butter
1 1/4 teaspoons	Baking soda
2 cups	Self rising flour, sifted

Preheat your oven to 350°F. Grease and flour 1-2 loaf pans.

Soak the banana pieces in the water for one hour.

Cream the butter and sugar, add the eggs and beat well. Drain the bananas pieces and add them with half of the milk and beat again. Add the rest of the milk, the peanut butter and the baking soda and flour. Beat until smooth.

Pour into the loaf pan(s) and bake for approximately one hour.

Banana Walnut Biscuits

3/4 cup	Dried banana pieces
1 cup	Hot water
1 1/2 cups	Flour
1 teaspoon	Baking powder
1 teaspoon	Ground cinnamon
1/4 teaspoon	Baking soda
1/4 teaspoon	Ground nutmeg
Pinch	Salt
1/4 cup	Sugar
13 tablespoons	Butter or margarine, softened
2	Eggs
1 1/2 cups	Rolled oats
1 1/2 cups	Walnuts or peanuts, chopped

Preheat your oven to 350°F. Grease a baking tray.

Soak the banana pieces in the hot water for one hour. Drain and purée.

Combine the flour, baking powder, cinnamon, baking soda, nutmeg and salt.

Add the sugar, butter or margarine, eggs and half of the puréed bananas. Beat until well mixed.

Fold in the remaining bananas, and the oats and walnuts.

Drop the batter by teaspoonfuls onto greased baking tray.

Bake for about 12-15 minutes or until firm and golden, Allow to cool slightly before removing them from the tray.

Bran Muffins

3 cups	Wheat or oat bran
1 cup	Boiling water
1/2 cup	Margarine, softened
2 cups	Buttermilk
2	Eggs, beaten
1 cup	Granulated sugar
1/2 cup	Brown sugar
2 1/2 cups	All purpose flour
2 1/2 teaspoons	Baking soda
2 teaspoons	Salt
1 cup	Dried apple, dates, raisins, pineapple, chopped
1/2 cup	Walnuts or pecans, chopped
1/4 cup	Raw sugar

Preheat your oven to 400°F. Fill 24 muffin pans with muffin liners and spray them lightly with vegetable spray.

In a large bowl, pour the boiling water over 1 cup of the bran and let it stand for a few minutes. Add the margarine and stir in the buttermilk, eggs, sugars and remaining bran.

In another bowl, combine the flour, baking soda, and salt. Add the chopped dried fruit and stir.

Combine the dry ingredients with the wet and stir only until moist. The batter should be lumpy. Spoon it into the muffin cups and sprinkle the coarse sugar on top.

Bake for 20-25 minutes. Remove from the pans to cool.

Cinnamon Blueberry Muffins

1 cup	Dried blueberries
1 cup	Warm water
1 cup	Low fat buttermilk
1 teaspoon	Baking powder
1/2 teaspoon	Salt
1 tablespoon	Vegetable oil
1 1/2 teaspoons	Cinnamon
3/4 cup	Brown sugar
1/2 cup	Water
4 large	Egg whites
3 1/2 cups	Oat bran

Preheat your oven to 400°F. Spray 12 muffin tins with vegetable spray or use muffin liners.

Soak the blueberries in the water for at least one hour until tender and drain.

Mix the buttermilk, baking powder, salt, oil, cinnamon, brown sugar and water. Allow to sit for 3 minutes until bubbly.

Whip the egg whites until soft peaks form and fold them into the buttermilk mixture. Fold the oat bran into the mixture just until blended. Stir in the drained blueberries.

Spoon the batter into the muffin tins and bake for 20 minutes until lightly browned and firm to the touch. Allow to cool for 5 minutes before removing the tins.

Date and Nut Bread

4 tablespoons	Butter, softened
1/2 cup	Brown sugar
1	Egg, lightly beaten
5 ounces	Milk
3/4 cup	Dried dates, chopped
1/2 cup	Walnuts, chopped
1 1/2 cups	Self rising flour

Preheat your oven to 350°F. Grease and flour 1-2 loaf pans.

Cream the butter and sugar and add the beaten egg.

Stir in the milk, dried dates and walnuts. Gently fold in the flour.

Pour the batter into the pan(s) and bake for 30-40 minutes.

Remove the bread and allow it to cool before slicing.

It is delicious served warm or cold with butter or cream cheese.

Dried Fruit Pancakes

1 cup	Dried blueberries or other fruit
1 cup	Grape juice or water
2 cups	Pancake mix

Soak the blueberries in the grape juice or water for at least one hour or as long as overnight. Drain when ready for use.

Make the pancake mix according to the directions and add the drained blueberries. Cook as usual.

Notes: You can use practically any dried fruit that sounds good to you. I made the one pictured at the start of this section with dried cranberries. Be aware, cranberries take a long time to dry.

Herb Scones

2 cups	Self rising flour
2 tablespoons	Butter or margarine, softened
1 tablespoon	Sugar
Pinch	Salt
2 teaspoons	Dried herbs
2/3 cup	Milk

Preheat your oven to 400°F and grease a cookie tray.

Mix all of the ingredients except the milk until crumbly.

Mix in the milk gradually until a soft dough ball forms. Turn the dough out onto floured board and knead lightly.

Roll the dough to 1/4 inch thickness and cut with a floured scone cutter.

Place close together on the greased tray and glaze with milk if desired.

Bake for 10-12 minutes until golden brown.

Note: If you prefer, you can get a scone pan for making perfectly shaped cones. Nordic Ware makes one that has gotten a lot of good reviews.

Waffles

2	Eggs, separated
2 1/2 cups	Buttermilk
1/2 cup	Vegetable oil
1 1/2 cups	All purpose flour
1 1/2 cups	Corn meal
2 teaspoons	Baking powder
2 teaspoons	Baking soda
1 teaspoon	Salt
1/2 cup	Dried apple, pineapple or apricots, finely chopped

Preheat your waffle iron.

In a small bowl, beat the egg whites until stiff and set aside.

In a medium bowl, beat the egg yolks, buttermilk, and vegetable oil until well mixed.

In large bowl, combine the flour, corn meal, baking powder, baking soda, and salt. Add the dried fruit and stir.

Add the liquid ingredients to the dry and stir only until well combined and moist.

Pour the batter onto the hot waffle iron and bake as directed by the waffle iron.

Serve hot with syrup, jam, or yogurt.

Zucchini Bread

1 cup	Dried zucchini, powdered
3/4 cup	Warm water
3 cups	All purpose flour
3 teaspoons	Baking powder
1 teaspoon	Salt
1 teaspoon	Cinnamon
1 cup	Vegetable oil
3	Eggs
2 cups	Sugar
2 teaspoons	Vanilla
1/2 cup	Walnuts or pecans, chopped (optional)

Preheat your oven to 325°F. Grease and flour 1-2 loaf pans.

Mix the water and zucchini powder together and let stand for a few minutes.

Combine the flour, baking powder, salt and cinnamon and set it aside.

Combine the oil, eggs, sugar and vanilla and stir until well mixed.

Add the wet mixture to the dry and mix well. Add in the zucchini with remainder of the ingredients to get a somewhat lumpy batter. Add the walnuts or pecans, if desired.

Pour the batter into the loaf pans and bake for one hour or until a toothpick comes out clean.

Cereals

Apple Granola

1 tablespoon	Honey
1/4 cup	Water
3 medium	Granny Smith apples, peeled, cored and coarsely grated
2 cups	Quick cooking oatmeal
1/2 cup	Slivered almonds
2 tablespoons	Brown sugar
1 teaspoon	Salt
1/2 teaspoon	Cinnamon

Dissolve the honey in the water. Add all of the other ingredients and mix well.

Pour the mixture on solid fruit roll sheets on your dehydrator trays. Dry for 2-3 hours or until crunchy. Store in an air-tight container.

Note: For a softer granola, add 1/4 cup of vegetable oil before drying.

Apricot Raisin Granola

4 cups	Old fashioned oatmeal
1/2 cup	Vegetable oil
1/2 cup	Brown sugar
1/2 cup	Sunflower seeds
1/2 cup	Almonds, sliced
1/2 cup	Dried apricots, chopped
1/2 cup	Raisins

Combine the oatmeal, oil and brown sugar. Toss gently until well blended.

Add the sunflower seeds and almonds. Mix well.

Spread the mixture about 1/2" thick on solid fruit roll sheets on your dehydrator trays.

Dry 4-7 hours until crunchy. Add the apricots and raisins and store in an air-tight container.

Notes: For the best results, do not use quick or rolled oats. You can add more sugar for sweeter granola if desired.

Dried Fruit Oatmeal

1 cup	Old fashioned oatmeal
2 cups	Milk or water
1/4 teaspoon	Salt
1/2 teaspoon	Ground cinnamon
1 tablespoon	Margarine or butter (optional)
1 cup	Dried fruit of choice

Mix together all of the ingredients in a bowl and pour into a slow cooker. If desired, spray the inside of the slow cooker with cooking spray first so the oatmeal won't stick. Cook on the low setting overnight.

Notes: Use regular, slow cooking oatmeal, not the quick or instant kind.

This is the recipe pictured at the beginning of this section.

Harvest Granola

5 cups	Rolled oats
1/2 cup	Wheat germ
1/2-3/4 cup	Brown sugar
1/2 cup	Dried apple, chopped
1/2 cup	Sesame seeds
1 cup	Raisins
1/2 cup	Date Crystals®
1 teaspoon	Cinnamon
1 cup	Pecans or almonds, chopped
1/2 cup	Honey
1 teaspoon	Vanilla
3/4 cup	Margarine, melted

Combine the dry ingredients and mix well. Combine the wet ingredients separately. Add the dry mixture to the wet mixing well.

Spread the mixture on solid fruit roll sheets on your dehydrator trays. Dry until crunchy. Store in an airtight container.

A Note about Date Crystals®: Floyd Shields invented Date Crystals® in 1936. He and his wife Bess came to the California desert in 1924 and started Shields Date Garden to educate people about the date. Mr. Shields created several new varieties of dates and the Crystals which are about the size of oatmeal flakes. Their size and texture make them perfect for cooking.

For more information visit: http://www.shieldsdategarden.com

Muesli

2 cups	Rolled oats
1/4 cup	Vegetable oil
1/4 cup	Brown sugar
1/4 cup	Sunflower seeds
1/2 cup	Dried apricots, chopped
1/4 cup	Raisins

Combine the rolled oats, oil and brown sugar and mix well.

Spread the mixture on solid fruit roll sheets on your dehydrator trays. Dry approximately 10-12 hours.

Once it is dried to your desired consistency, add the apricots and raisins.

Store in an air tight container, in a cool spot.

Beverages

Banana Smoothie

1/2 cup	Dried banana pieces
1 (8 oz.) container	Yogurt
1 cup	Milk
1/4 teaspoon	Vanilla
1/2 teaspoon	Cinnamon (optional)
	Honey (to taste)
1-2 cups	Crushed ice

Place the banana pieces, yogurt, milk, vanilla and cinnamon in a blender and blend until smooth. Add the honey and blend again. Add the ice and blend until the smoothie reaches your desired consistency.

This will make about 3 cups.

Note: You can use any dried fruit instead of bananas.

Fruit Leather Smoothie

1 cup	Fruit leather
1 cup	Water
	Ice cubes
	Ginger ale
	Sugar/grenadine syrup to taste (optional)

Purée the fruit leather with the water in a blender. Let it stand for 15 minutes and purée again.

Fill a tall glass with ice cubes and add enough of the fruit purée to fill the glass two thirds full. Add the ginger ale and stir.

Sweeten to taste with grenadine syrup or sugar syrup if desired.

Notes: If you made your fruit leather without reading my tip about not being stingy, this is a terrific use for the fruit leather crumbs! Nothing needs to go to waste.

This is the drink pictured at the beginning of this section.

These are dried Vidalia onions in this picture.

Vegetables

Creamed Vegetables

2 cups	Dried vegetables, sliced or diced
2 1/2 cups	Boiling water
	Milk
1/4 cup	Butter
3 tablespoons	Flour
1	Bay leaf
	Salt and Pepper

Combine the dried vegetables with boiling water to reconstitute. Cover and let them stand 1-2 hours. As an alternative you can use cold water and reconstitute them overnight in your refrigerator.

Simmer the vegetables until tender, adding more water if necessary. When cooked, drain the water into a measuring cup and add enough milk to equal 1 cup.

Melt the butter in a saucepan, add the flour and cook, stirring until bubbly and smooth.

Remove the butter/flour from the heat and stir in the cup of water/milk. Add the bay leaf and cook, stirring constantly, until the cream sauce thickens.

Add the drained vegetables and simmer for 5 minutes longer.

Remove the bay leaf and season with salt and pepper before serving.

Note: You can use any combination of dried green beans, peas, carrots, parsnips, broccoli, Brussels sprouts, or cauliflower.

Creamed Vegetable Casserole

3/4 cup	Cheddar cheese, grated
1/4 teaspoon	Dry mustard
1/2 cup	Dry bread crumbs
3 tablespoons	Butter, melted

Prepare the Creamed Vegetables recipe leaving out the bay leaf.

Preheat your oven to 350°F. Grease a 2 quart baking dish.

Add the cheese and mustard to the vegetables and pour them into the baking dish. Combine the bread crumbs and melted butter and mix until crumbly. Sprinkle the mixture over the vegetables.

Bake for 30-35 minutes until browned.

Dried Tomatoes

7 pounds	Firm, ripe Roma or plum tomatoes, cleaned, stems removed
1 teaspoon	Dried basil
1 teaspoon	Dried oregano
1 teaspoon	Dried thyme
2 teaspoons	Salt

Cut the tomatoes in half and scrape out all of the seeds without removing the pulp. Sprinkle the seasonings over the tomatoes and place them cut side up on the dehydrator racks.

Dry for a total of 6-9 hours. At about 3 hours check them and gently turn them over and press them flat with your hand or a spatula. Repeat this step again in a few hours until dried. They should be dry and leathery with no moisture, but not crisp.

Marinated Tomatoes (Version 1)

2 tablespoons	Dried tomatoes
1 1/2 tablespoons	Olive oil
1/2 tablespoon	Fresh basil, finely chopped
1/2 tablespoon	Fresh oregano, finely chopped

Combine all ingredients in a bowl and mix well. Use as a garnish or on a salad.

Note: Be careful about storing tomatoes in oil. You can store them for several weeks but be sure there is no moisture in the dried tomatoes, they are covered totally in oil and stored in a glass jar in a cool, dark place. It's safest to prepare them just before you use them.

Marinated Tomatoes (Version 2)

2 tablespoons	Dried tomato slices
	Red or White wine vinegar
	Extra light olive oil

Dip the dried tomato slices in the vinegar and then the oil. Shake off any excess. Use as a garnish or on a salad.

Marinated Peppers

6 tablespoons	Dried red pepper slices
6 tablespoons	Dried green pepper slices
1 cup	Vegetable oil
1 tablespoon	Dried oregano, finely chopped
1 tablespoon	Dried basil, finely chopped
1 clove	Dried garlic, finely chopped

Combine all of the ingredients and mix well.

Store in an air tight jar, in a cool, dark place.

Tomato Powder

15 pounds	Ripe tomatoes
4 large	Green peppers
3 large	Onions
3 large	Carrots
2 cloves	Garlic
1 jar	Pimentos

Wash and core the tomatoes and peppers. Chop them in a blender or food processor. Chop the onions, carrots and garlic.

Combine the ingredients together and blend in a blender or food processor until smooth.

In a large saucepan bring the mixture to a boil over medium heat. Boil gently, uncovered for about 5 hours stirring often. Boil the mixture until it is thick enough to mound on a spoon.

Spoon the mixture on solid fruit roll sheets on your dehydrator trays and dry until crisp. Powder the dried mixture in the blender or food processor.

Add water to your tomato powder to make the following:
Tomato Paste
1 teaspoon powder with 1 teaspoon water

Tomato Sauce
1 teaspoon powder with 3 teaspoons water

Tomato Juice/Soup
1 teaspoon powder with 1/2 cup or more water. Adjust the amount of the water to taste for juice and soup.

Zucchini Bake

2 cups	Boiling water
2 cups	Dried zucchini slices
1 medium	Onion, thinly sliced
2 1/2 tablespoons	Vegetable oil
1 cup	Fresh or canned tomatoes
	Salt and pepper
1/2 cup	Mozzarella cheese, grated

Preheat your oven to 350°F. Grease a baking dish.

Pour the boiling water over the dried zucchini slices and allow them to sit for 1-2 hours. Drain.

Cook the onion slices in oil until transparent. Add the drained zucchini slices. Cook and stir for 5 minutes. Add the tomatoes and season to taste with salt and pepper.

Pour into the baking dish and top with the grated cheese. Bake for 25-30 minutes or until lightly browned.

Side Dishes

Herb Stuffing

2 tablespoons	Dried parsley
1/2 teaspoon	Dried sage
2 teaspoons	Dried chervil
2 (1 1/2 lb.)	Loaves of bread, cubed
1 teaspoon	Dried marjoram
1/2 cup	Butter
1 teaspoon	Dried savory
1/4 cup	Dried onion
1/4 cup	Celery
1/2 teaspoon	Dried thyme

Preheat your oven to 325°F.

Mix all ingredients, plus the chicken or turkey juice from the roasting pan or other liquid, to moisten.

Bake covered for one hour. Makes about 2 quarts.

Scalloped Potatoes (Version 1)

4 cups	Dried, sliced or grated potatoes
2 cups	Boiling water
1 1/2 cups	Cheddar or mozzarella cheese, grated
1 cup	Milk
1/2 teaspoon	Dried onion
1/2 teaspoon	Salt
1 teaspoon	Butter

Pour the boiling water over the dried potatoes and allow them to sit for one hour. Drain.

Preheat your oven to 350°F. Grease an 8 x 10 baking dish with butter.

Place half of the potatoes in the baking dish. Top with a layer of half of the cheese. Add the remaining potatoes on top. Add the onion and salt to the milk and pour over the layered potatoes and cheese.

Dot the top with butter and add the remaining cheese. Bake for 30 minutes or until tender.

Scalloped Potatoes (Version 2)

2 cups	Dried potato slices or cubes
1/4 cup	Dried onion
1 (13 oz.) can	Evaporated milk
1 1/2 cups	Cheddar or jack cheese, grated
1 (8 oz.) container	Sour cream
1 (10 3/4 oz.) can	Cream of chicken soup
1/4 cup	Butter, melted (optional)
	Milk (optional)

Preheat your oven to 350°F. Grease a 9x13 baking dish.

Soak the dried potatoes and onions in the evaporated milk for one hour. Drain, reserving any evaporated milk not absorbed.

Combine the potatoes, 1 cup of the cheese, the sour cream, soup and evaporated milk and mix well. If mixture is too thick add a little bit of regular milk.

Pour the ingredients in the baking dish. Top with the remaining cheese and melted butter. Cover with aluminum foil and bake for 30 minutes or until the cheese has melted and the potatoes are completely cooked. The foil can be removed the last 5 minutes so the top browns.

Note: This is the recipe pictured at the beginning of this section right out of the oven!

Sweet Potatoes

1 1/2 cups	Dried sweet potato strips
1 1/2 cups	Boiling water
1	Egg, well beaten
1/2 cup	Dry bread crumbs
	Vegetable oil or spray

Pour the boiling water over the potato strips. Allow them to soak for one hour. Drain and wipe the strips. Dip them in the beaten egg, then coat in bread crumbs.

Fry the strips in oil until golden brown.

Soups

Instant

Combine a combination of your favorite dried vegetables, dry rice or noodles and your favorite dried meat. Place into an airtight container until ready to use.

Preparation
Pour 2 cups of dried mix into 2 cups of boiling water. Cover and simmer until tender. Add seasonings to taste.

Note: This soup can cook in your thermos so it's ready to eat by lunch time.

Put the dried mix into your thermos and pour the boiling water over it. Close the cover securely.

French Onion

1 cup	Dried onion
1 cup	Water
1 cube	Beef bouillon
2 tablespoons	Butter
2 tablespoons	Flour
1/4 teaspoon	Salt

In a large saucepan, cook the onion in the water over a medium heat for 15 minutes or until it is soft. Drain the liquid and set it aside.

Brown the onions in the butter. Add the flour and salt, stir and add the broth. Add an additional 3 cups of water and simmer.

When ready to serve, pour the soup into individual oven safe bowls. Top each with toasted croutons and sprinkle with parmesan cheese.

Bake at 375°F long enough to melt and brown the cheese. Serve hot.

Note: You can substitute 1/2 cup beef stock for the bouillon and half of the water.

Mushroom

1 1/2 cups	Dried Mushrooms
1/2 cup	Dried Onions
1/4 cup	Margarine
2 cups	Hot beef bouillon
4 cups	Milk
1 teaspoon	Salt
6 tablespoons	Flour
	Parsley for garnish

Sauté the mushrooms and onions in the margarine in a heavy saucepan for 5 minutes, stirring occasionally.

Combine the bouillon, milk, salt and flour and mix until smooth. Add to the sautéed mushrooms and onions and cook, stirring constantly for 2-3 minutes longer.

Serve garnished with the parsley.

Vegetable (Version 1)

1/3 cup	Dried vegetables (any combination of tomatoes, peas, onions, broccoli, zucchini, celery, carrots)
1/4 teaspoon	Dried parsley
1/4 teaspoon	Dried sweet basil
Pinch	Garlic powder
Pinch	Onion powder
	Salt and pepper to taste
1 tablespoon	Bulgur wheat
1 tablespoon	Small pasta
2 cups	Boiling hot chicken or beef broth

This is another soup that you can cook in your thermos so it's ready to eat by lunch time.

Put the dried vegetables in a blender or food processor and whirl until they reach the size of small peas.

Remeasure the vegetables and put 1/3 cup of them in a pint thermos. Reserve any leftover vegetables for later or another use.

Add the parsley, basil, garlic and onion powders, salt and pepper. Add the bulgur wheat and pasta.

Bring the broth to a rolling boil and pour over dry ingredients. Close the cover securely.

Vegetable (Version 2)

2 cups	Dried diced beef (optional)
1/2 cup	Dried diced onions
1/2 cup	Dried diced carrots
2 tablespoons	Dried parsley, chopped
1/4 cup	Dried peas
1 cup	Dried tomatoes
1/2 cup	Pearl barley
1/2 cup	Dried diced celery and celery leaves
8 cups	Cold water
1 cup	Dried diced potatoes
1/4 teaspoon	Sage
	Salt and pepper to taste

Put the meat and vegetables in a soup pot and cover with the cold water. Bring almost to a boil, reduce the heat and simmer for four to six hours until the vegetables are tender.

One hour before serving, add the dried potatoes and sage. Season to taste with salt and pepper. Continue to cook for one hour.

Notes: If you use the beef, pre-cook the meat before dehydrating. You can either use leftover roast or get thin sliced flank steak and par boil until cooked.

The ingredients for this soup are pictured at the beginning of this section.

Vegetable (Version 3)

1 cup	Dried tomatoes
1 cup	Dried carrots
1 cup	Dried beans
1 cup	Dried celery
1 cup	Dried peas
4 cups	Water
	Dried parsley

Cover the vegetables with the water in a soup pot. Add the parsley and bring to a boil, stirring frequently.

Cover and simmer for about 2 hours or until the vegetables are soft.

Note: You can adjust the amount of water you use to get a thicker or thinner soup.

Vegetable (Version 4)

1/2 cup	Dried sliced potatoes
1/4 cup	Dried green beans
1/4 cup	Dried sliced carrots
2 tablespoons	Dried chopped onion
4 cups	Water
5	Dried tomato slices
3 tablespoons	Dried green peas
1 tablespoon	Dried okra, optional
1 tablespoon	Dried parsley
1/2 teaspoon	Dried thyme
1/2 teaspoon	Salt
1/4 teaspoon	Pepper

Combine the potatoes, green beans, carrots and onion with the water in a soup pot. Bring the soup to a boil and remove from the heat. Cover the pot and let it stand 3 hours or overnight.

Bring the soup to almost a boil and simmer it for 30 minutes. Add the remaining vegetables and additional water if needed for the desired thickness. Continue to cook for about 30 minutes or until the vegetables are tender. Add seasonings and simmer for 10 minutes longer. Makes approximately 5 cups.

Variations:
Minestrone

1/2 cup	Dried kidney or navy beans or chickpeas
5 additional	Dried tomato slices
1/4 cup	Dried zucchini slices
1/4 cup	Shredded cabbage
1/2 cup	Dried spinach
1/2 teaspoon	Dried oregano
1/2 teaspoon	Worcestershire sauce

Omit the potatoes and add the above ingredients. Increase the final cooking time from 10 to 20 minutes and season to taste with the salt, pepper and Worcestershire sauce.

Beef or Chicken Stew

2 cups	Dried cubed beef or chicken
1 cup additional	Dried sliced potatoes
2 tablespoons	Flour
1/2 cup	Cold water

Prepare the Vegetable Soup as directed, adding the dried meat and extra potatoes to the vegetables in the first step.

During the last 10 minutes of cooking time, stir together the flour and cold water and pour it into the stew, stirring constantly, until thickened. Cover and continue to simmer until the desired consistency is reached.

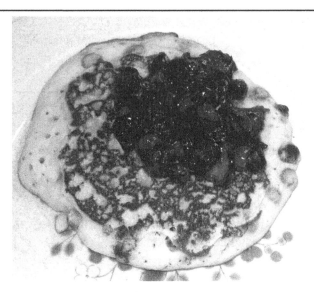

Sauces

Fruit Sauce

3 cups	Dried strawberries
1/2 cup	Dried banana chips
1 cup	Dried blueberries or raspberries
1 cup	Warm water
1/2 cup	Maple syrup
1/3 cup	Oat bran (optional)

Put the dried fruit and water in a saucepan and simmer over medium heat until tender. Add the maple syrup and oat bran. Let the sauce cool and serve warm over pancakes or waffles.

Notes: You can serve this as is or for a smoother sauce, put the cooled sauce into a blender or food processor. Blend until reaching the desired consistency, adding more water if necessary.

The picture above is the pancake made with dried cranberries pictured in the Baked Goods/Breakfast section with the fruit sauce on top. Yummy!

Spaghetti Sauce

2 tablespoons	Dried bell pepper
3 tablespoons	Dried onion
1 dried	Bay leaf
1 cup	Dried tomato slices
3/4 cup	Dried mushroom pieces
1 teaspoon	Salt
1/2-1 teaspoon	Pepper
1/2 teaspoon	Sugar
1 can (18 oz.)	Tomato paste
4 1/2 cups	Water
3 cloves	Fresh garlic, chopped
1 teaspoon	Dried oregano
1/2-1 teaspoon	Dried basil
2 tablespoon	Olive oil
1 pound	Ground beef
2 stalks	Fresh celery, chopped
	Parmesan cheese

Combine the pepper, onion, bay leaf, tomato, mushroom, salt, pepper, sugar, tomato paste and water and mix well. Let it sit for 2-3 hours.

In a large skillet, sauté the garlic, oregano and basil in the olive oil. Add the ground beef and cook until browned. Remove from the heat and drain.

In another skillet, cook the vegetables over medium heat until they are tender, approximately 20-30 minutes.

Combine the vegetables and meat mixture and heat. Add the chopped celery 10 minutes before serving.

Serve over spaghetti noodles and top with Parmesan cheese.

Sweet and Sour

1/4 cup	Dried pineapple pieces
3/4 cup	Water
3 tablespoons	Vegetable oil
1 tablespoon	Soy sauce
1/4 cup	Vinegar
1/4 teaspoon	Dried ginger
2 tablespoons	Sugar
1 teaspoon	Cornstarch

Combine everything except the cornstarch in a small saucepan. Cook over medium heat until the pineapple softens.

Place the mixture in a blender or food processor and purée. Add the cornstarch and blend again.

Return the purée to the pan and cook over medium heat until mixture thickens.

Tomato Paste

4 quarts	Ripe tomatoes
1 teaspoon	Fresh oregano
1/2 cup	Carrots, chopped
1/4 teaspoon	Garlic powder
1/3 cup	Onions, chopped
1/3 cup	Celery, chopped
2 tablespoons	Basil leaves
1 teaspoon	Salt

In a large saucepan, cook all of the ingredients over low heat until the vegetables are tender. Add a little water if necessary.

Strain the cooked vegetables through a sieve or process in a blender or food processor until smooth. Return the purée to the saucepan and simmer until thick.

Spread on solid fruit roll sheets on your dehydrator trays.

Dry for 10-12 hours or until there is no moisture left. Roll the mixture like fruit leather and wrap in fresh plastic wrap. Store the rolls in your refrigerator or freezer for rehydrating later.

To rehydrate: Place the tomato rolls in a container with enough water to cover them. Let them sit for 30 minutes to 2 hours. You can use boiling water to rehydrate them more quickly.

Spice Mixtures

Chili Powder

3 ounces	Dried chilies (mild, or a combination of mild and hot)
1 tablespoon	Ground cumin
2 teaspoons	Salt
1 teaspoon	Ground allspice
1 teaspoon	Garlic powder
1 teaspoon	Onion powder
1 teaspoon	Ground oregano
1/2 teaspoon	Ground cloves
1 teaspoon	Ground coriander

Remove and discard the stems and seeds of the chilies. Process them in a blender or food processor until finely ground. Allow the powder to settle and add the remaining ingredients. Process again until combined. Makes 1/2 cup.

Store the powder in an airtight container.

Notes: If you'd like you can make most of the spices listed yourself. Dehydrate the vegetables and herbs and then process to powder just like you do the chilies.

Use this powder in your favorite Mexican recipe or in ground meat for tacos.

Herb Blend (Version 1)

1 tablespoon	Dried Oregano
1 tablespoon	Dried Marjoram
1 tablespoon	Dried Basil
2 teaspoons	Dried Summer Savory
1 teaspoon	Dried Rosemary
1 teaspoon	Dried Sage

Combine all the herbs in a glass jar and mix well. Close the jar with a tight-fitting lid and store in a cool, dark place.

Uses include flavoring soups, stews, or vegetable dishes. For the most flavorful results, use your own freshly picked, home grown herbs and dry them right before making this blend.

Herb Blend (Version 2)

2 tablespoons	Dried parsley
2	Bay leaves
1 teaspoon	Dried rosemary
1 teaspoon	Dried thyme
1 teaspoon	Dried tarragon

Combine the herbs in a bowl and mix well. Place them in the center of a 4-inch square of cheesecloth. Gather the corners and twist them closed. Tie the square closed with string. Drop the bag into cooking soup or stew. Remove before serving.

Herb Butter

1/2 cup	Butter or margarine, softened
1 tablespoon	Dried dill, oregano, basil and tarragon
1 tablespoon	Lemon juice
	Salt and pepper to taste

In small bowl, cream the butter or margarine. Slowly add the lemon juice stirring until combined. Add the herbs, salt and pepper and mix well. Cover and refrigerate until ready to use.

Note: This makes an excellent spread for your homemade bread! It's pictured at the beginning of this section.

Seasoned Salt

4 tablespoons	Dried onions and/or garlic, powdered
1 tablespoon	Salt

Mix the ingredients well and store in shaker bottle in a cool, dark place.

Salads

Salad Topping (Version 1)

1/2 cup	Dried onions
1/2 cup	Dried carrots
1/2 cup	Dried tomatoes
1/2 cup	Dried bell pepper
1/4 cup	Roasted sunflower seeds
1 tablespoon	Basil or oregano

Combine the ingredients and mix well. If some of the vegetables are too large, you can break them into smaller pieces. Add as much as desired on the top of salads after adding the salad dressing. Store any leftover in your refrigerator in baggies.

Note: One of my favorite salad toppings is Vidalia onion, pictured above. It retains its sweetness after drying and is very crunchy.

Salad Topping (Version 2)

1/2 cup	Dried onions
1/2 cup	Dried carrots
1/2 cup	Dried tomatoes
1/2 cup	Dried peppers
1/2 cup	Bacon bits
1/4 cup	Roasted sunflower seeds
1/4 cup	Soy nuts

Combine the ingredients and mix well. If some of the vegetables are too large, you can break them into smaller pieces. Add as much as desired on the top of salads after adding the salad dressing.

Store any leftover in your refrigerator in baggies.

Note: The carrots pictured at the start of this section are pre-packaged matchstick carrots. They dehydrate into very thin strings and are wonderful on salads. The easiest way to dehydrate these is on mesh screens on your trays. They don't fall through as easily and it doesn't take as long to spread them out.

Complete Meals

Goulash

1 1/2 pounds	Lean ground turkey
1 cup	Onion, chopped
1 tablespoon	Vegetable oil
1 teaspoon	Garlic, fresh
1 teaspoon	Salt
1/2 teaspoon	Oregano, dried
1/2 teaspoon	Black pepper
1 (28 oz.) can	Tomatoes, chopped
1 (7 oz.) package	Shell or elbow macaroni

In a frying pan sauté the turkey and onion in the oil on high heat until completely cooked. Stir often to break the turkey into small pieces. Add the seasonings and tomatoes, reduce the heat to medium low and cook until most of liquid has evaporated.

Remove from the heat and allow to cool. Lightly oil two solid fruit roll sheets and spread the mixture on evenly.

Dehydrate for 6 hours or until everything is completely dry.

Place in air-tight container and refrigerate. It can be stored for up to 6 months.

To Make the Goulash:
Put the dehydrated meat mixture in a saucepan, add 2 cups of boiling water, stir, cover and allow it to sit for at least 30 minutes. Remove the cover and cook over medium heat for about 5 minutes stirring occasionally.

In a separate pan, cook the macaroni according to package directions. Add meat mixture to cooked pasta. Stir and serve.

Notes: This is a great backpacking meal. The ingredients are extremely lightweight and easy to pack.

Lean ground beef can be substituted for ground turkey.

Hot Dog Stew

8 cups	Soup stock or water
1 (8 oz.) package	Small pasta
3	Hot Dogs, finely chopped
1	Bell Pepper, minced (optional)
3 cups	Spaghetti sauce
1 tablespoon	Cayenne pepper (optional)
1/2 cup	Parmesan cheese, finely grated

In a large pot bring the stock or water to a rolling boil. Stir in pasta, return to a boil and add the hot dogs and bell pepper. Cook for 7 minutes or until the pasta is tender. Do not drain.

Stir in the spaghetti sauce and cayenne pepper. Remove from the heat and stir in the Parmesan cheese and allow it to cool. It will thicken as it cools.

Spread the cooled mixture onto solid fruit roll sheets on your dehydrator trays. Dehydrate for approximately 6-8 hours.

To Make the Stew:
Put the dehydrated mixture in a saucepan and cover with water to just above level of food. Boil and serve.

Notes: This could also be a great backpacking meal option. Package the dehydrated mixture in plastic baggies to carry.

This recipe makes a lot of stew! If you have only two solid fruit roll sheets, you'll want to cut the recipe in half. Or you can make it all, dehydrate half of it and eat the rest for dinner!

Go easy on the cayenne pepper if you don't like spicy dishes.

This recipe is pictured at the beginning of the section.

Jerky Marinades

For these marinades, combine the ingredients in bowl and mix well. Let the mixture sit at least 15 minutes so the flavors will blend.

Add the meat, sliced into 1/4" thin strips, and let it sit for at least 30 minutes, turning occasionally. If you would like to let it marinate longer, put it in the refrigerator in a covered container or in an air-tight plastic bag.

Any extra instructions are included with the individual recipes.

When ready to dry your jerky, remove the meat from the marinade and let it drain for a few minutes. Dehydrate for approximately 6-12 hours until chewy.

Barbecue

2 tablespoons	Brown sugar
2 tablespoons	White sugar
1 tablespoon	Oil
1/4 cup	Onion, minced
1 cup	Beer
2/3 cup	Ketchup
2 tablespoons	Cider vinegar
2 tablespoons	Worcestershire sauce
2 tablespoons	Ground ginger
1 teaspoon	Salt
1 teaspoon	Garlic, minced
1 teaspoon	Dijon mustard
1 teaspoon	Liquid smoke
1/2 teaspoon	Ground black pepper
Dash	Cayenne pepper
1 pound	Lean beef strips

In a frying pan, combine the sugars, oil, and onion and heat, stirring occasionally until the onions caramelize. Add the beer and simmer.

Cool the mixture and add the remaining ingredients except for the meat. Let the mixture sit at least 15 minutes so the flavors will blend, then purée in blender or food processor.

Add the meat strips and marinate at least one hour before dehydrating.

Beef

4 tablespoons	Soy sauce
4 tablespoons	Worcestershire sauce
1 tablespoons	Tomato sauce
1 tablespoon	Ginger root, grated (optional)
1/4 teaspoon	Black pepper (more for hotter jerky)
1 tablespoon	Curry powder (optional)
2 cloves	Garlic, chopped
1/2 teaspoon	Salt
1 pound	Lean beef strips

Note: You can also use this recipe on venison or other game meats.

Burgundy

2 cups	Burgundy wine
1/2 cup	Soy sauce
3 cloves	Garlic, chopped
3 tablespoons	Molasses
1 tablespoon	Black pepper, ground
1 pound	Lean meat strips

Cajun

1 cup	Tomato juice
1/2 teaspoon	Garlic powder
1/2 teaspoon	Ground black pepper
1 1/2 teaspoons	Dried thyme
1 1/2 teaspoons	Dried basil
1 1/2 teaspoons	Onion pepper
1 teaspoon	White pepper
2 teaspoons	Cayenne pepper (or more to taste)
1 pound	Lean meat strips

For Beef, Fish or Turkey

3cups	Soy sauce
1 cup	Brown sugar
1 cup	Liquid smoke
1-2 pounds	Lean meat strips

For this one you can let it marinate for 3 hours or overnight in an airtight container.

For Turkey

1/4 cup	Soy sauce
1 tablespoon	Fresh lemon juice
1/4 teaspoon	Garlic powder
1/4 teaspoon	Pepper
1/8 teaspoon	Ginger
1 1/2 pounds	Turkey breast strips

For Venison

1/3 cup	Soy sauce
1 tablespoon	Brown sugar
1 teaspoon	Salt
1/2 teaspoon	Garlic, minced
1/2 teaspoon	Ground black pepper
1 pound	Venison strips

Hawaiian

1 teaspoon	Salt
1 teaspoon	Ground ginger
1/4 cup	Pineapple juice
1 tablespoon	Brown sugar
1/4 teaspoon	Pepper
1/8 teaspoon	Cayenne pepper
1 clove	Garlic, crushed
1/4 cup	Soy sauce
1 pound	Lean meat strips

Hot Teriyaki

1/3 cup	Teriyaki sauce
2 teaspoons	Brown sugar
2 teaspoons	Ground black pepper
1 teaspoon	Horseradish, ground
1 teaspoon	Salt
1/2 teaspoon	Paprika
1/2 teaspoon	Chili powder
1 tablespoon	Olive oil
1 tablespoon	Garlic, minced
1/4 teaspoon	Tabasco sauce
2 tablespoons	Jalapeño peppers, seeded and chopped
1 pound	Lean meat strips

Soy Sauce

1/4 cup	Soy sauce
2 tablespoons	Honey
1/2 teaspoon	Dry mustard
1/4 teaspoon	Garlic powder
1 1/2 pounds	Lean meat strips

Snacks

Apple and Cheese Crackers

1 1/4 cups	Whole wheat flour
1/2 teaspoon	Cinnamon
1/2 teaspoon	Salt
1/2 teaspoon	Onion powder
1/3 cup	Butter, softened
1 1/2 cups	Cheddar cheese, grated
1 1/4 cups	Walnuts, ground
1 cup	Tart green apple, grated

Combine the flour, cinnamon, salt and onion powder and mix well. Stir in the butter and then add the cheese, walnuts and apple. Mix until well blended and form the dough into a ball.

Place the dough on a large sheet of waxed paper and shape into a log. Wrap it tightly with waxed paper and chill 4-6 hours or overnight.

Slice the dough into 1/4" rounds and put them on solid fruit roll sheets on your dehydrator trays. Dry for 4-6 hours or until firm and crisp. Store in an air-tight container. Makes approximately 50 crackers.

Apple Slices (Version 1)

Apples, peeled, cored and sliced
Lemon, orange or grapefruit juice

Slice the apples so they are the same thickness. Dip the slices in the juice, let drain slightly and place on the dehydrator trays. Dehydrate until desired consistency.

Apple Slices (Version 2)

	Apples, peeled, cored and sliced
	Lemon, orange or grapefruit juice
1 package	Jello (any flavor)

Slice the apples so they are the same thickness. Dip the slices in the juice and then in the jello powder. Make sure both sides are coated. Place the slices on the dehydrator trays and dehydrate until desired consistency.

Note: This is the recipe pictured at the beginning of this section.

Apple Slices (Version 3)

4	Apples, peeled, cored and sliced
1/4 cup	Pineapple juice
1 tablespoon	Sugar
1 teaspoon	Ground cinnamon

Slice the apples so they are the same thickness. Dip the slices in pineapple juice, let drain slightly and place on the dehydrator trays.

Mix together the sugar and cinnamon and sprinkle on top of the apple slices. Dehydrate until desired consistency.

Apricot Raisin Granola Bars

1/4 cup	Brown sugar
1/2 cup	Peanut butter
3 tablespoons	Butter
1/4 cup	Water
2 cups	Apricot raisin granola (store bought or from the recipe on page 22)

In a small saucepan, heat the brown sugar, peanut butter, and butter until melted, stirring frequently. Remove from the heat and add the water and granola and mix well. Press the mixture into foil lined 9" pan and refrigerate one hour.

Cut the dough into bars and put them on your dehydrator trays. Dry 6-10 hours until chewy. To dry them faster, turn them over half way through the drying process.

Au Gratin Potato Chips

3 cups	Potatoes, peeled, boiled and mashed
1 1/2 cups	Sharp cheddar cheese, grated
1/2 cup	Parmesan cheese, grated
1/2 teaspoon	Salt

Put the ingredients in a blender or food processor and mix well. Spread the mixture on solid fruit roll sheets on your dehydrator trays. Dry for 4 hours.

With a butter knife, lift the entire ring off the sheet, turn it over and dry it for one more hour or until dry enough to break into pieces.

Banana Bars

1 cup	Dried pineapple, finely chopped
1 cup	Dried apricots, finely chopped
1 cup	Dried peaches, finely chopped
1 cup	Ripe bananas, mashed
1/2 cup	Walnuts, crushed
1/2 cup	Whole grain cereal flakes
3 tablespoons	Pineapple juice

Combine all of the ingredients and mix well. Form the mixture into bars and put them on solid fruit roll sheets on your dehydrator trays Dry for one hour and remove from the trays.

Cut the bars into 1" squares, put them back on the dehydrator trays and dry them for another 3 hours or until the squares hold together. Makes about 2 dozen.

Banana Cinnamon Chips

Ripe bananas
Lemon or fruit juice
Sugar
Cinnamon

Slice the bananas so they are the same thickness. Dip the slices in the juice, let them drain slightly and place them on the dehydrator trays.

Mix together the sugar and cinnamon and sprinkle on top of the slices. Dehydrate until desired consistency.

Candied Fruit

Rinse the fruit of your choice and cut it into thin strips. Simmer slowly in approximately 2 cups of water and 2 cups sugar for 1 1/2 hours or until tender.

Put the slices on your dehydrator trays and dry until leathery.

Cool and store in air tight containers or baggies in your refrigerator. Use for snacks or in cooking.

Candied Strawberries

1 pound	Fresh strawberries
1 (3 oz.) package	Strawberry Jello
1/2 cup	Powdered sugar

Slice the strawberries about 3/8" thick. Sprinkle lightly with the dry strawberry gelatin and then with the powdered sugar.

Dry for 4 hours or until crisp.

Variation:
Replace the Jello and sugar with

1/4 cup	Honey
1/4 cup	Lemon juice

Combine the honey and lemon juice and mix well. Dip the strawberry slices in the mixture and place on your dehydrator trays.

Dry for 4 hours or until crisp.

Caramel Corn

1 cup	Butter or margarine
2 cups	Brown sugar
1/2 cup	Light corn syrup
1 teaspoon	Salt
1/2 teaspoon	Baking soda
1 teaspoon	Vanilla
6 cups	Popped popcorn
2 cups	Dried fruit, finely chopped

Preheat your oven to 250°F. Grease a shallow 11" x 14" baking dish.

In a large saucepan, melt the butter or margarine. Stir in the brown sugar, syrup, and salt. Bring the mixture to a boil, stirring constantly, then boil for 5 minutes without stirring.

Remove from the heat and stir in the baking soda and vanilla. Be aware it may foam. Pour the mixture over the popped corn and mix well.

Pour the popcorn into the baking dish and bake for one hour, stirring every 20 minutes. During last 5 minutes stir in the dried fruit.

Remove from oven, cool, and break apart. Makes 7 cups of caramel corn.

Note: Dried pineapple, apple, raisins and prunes are good choices for the fruit in this recipe.

Caraway Rye Crackers

1 1/4 cups	Rye flour
1/2 teaspoon	Salt
1 1/2 teaspoons	Caraway seeds
1/2 cup	Butter or margarine, softened
1 cup	Swiss cheese, grated
1 cup	Sauerkraut, drained and squeezed dry

Combine the flour, salt, and caraway seeds. Add the butter, cheese and sauerkraut. Mix until well blended.

Form the dough into a ball. Place it on a large sheet of waxed paper and shape it into a log. Wrap the waxed paper tightly around the dough and chill it for 4-6 hours or overnight.

With a sharp knife, slice the dough into 1/4" rounds. Place them on solid fruit roll sheets on your dehydrator trays and dry for 4-6 hours or until firm and crisp.

Store in an air-tight container. Makes approximately 50 crackers.

Cherry Pineapples

1 can   Pineapple rings, any size
1 jar   Maraschino cherries, any size

Drain the pineapple rings and cherries and put them on paper towels for a few minutes to absorb any extra liquid.

Put the pineapple rings on your dehydrator trays with a cherry in center of each.

Dry 8-10 hours.

Chili Peanuts

1 (16 oz.) jar   Dry roasted, unsalted peanuts
1/2 cup   Water
1/4 cup   Tabasco sauce
1 1/2 tablespoons   Chili powder
1 teaspoon   Ground cumin
1/2 teaspoon   Red pepper
1/8 teaspoon   Ground oregano

Put the nuts in a 9" square pan or dish. Combine the rest of the ingredients in a bowl and mix well. Pour the mixture over the nuts at let them sit overnight at room temperature.

Drain the liquid from the nuts and put them on mesh screens on your dehydrator trays.

Dry for 3-5 hours or until the nuts are crunchy. Store in an airtight container.

Corn Chips

1 cup	Whole kernel or creamed corn
1 cup	Sharp cheddar cheese, grated
1/2 cup	Red or green peppers, diced
1 tablespoon	Onion, chopped
1/8 teaspoon	Cayenne pepper
1/8 teaspoon	Chili powder
	Salt to taste

Combine all of the ingredients in a blender or food processor until well mixed.

Spread the mixture thinly onto solid fruit roll sheets on your dehydrator trays. Dry for approximately 10 hours or until dry on one side. Lift the entire ring off the fruit roll sheet, turn it over, and dry it for two hours longer or until crisp.

Break into pieces.

Cottage Cheese Chips

1 (12 oz.) carton	Cottage cheese with chives
1 medium	Ripe tomato, quartered
1 tablespoon	Onion, chopped
Dash	Cayenne pepper
Dash	Garlic powder

Combine the cottage cheese, tomato, onion and spices in a blender or food processor and process until smooth.

Pour the mixture by spoonfuls onto solid fruit roll sheets on your dehydrator trays. Dry for 4-6 hours or until they are crispy like potato chips.

Date and Fig Balls

1 cup	Dried dates
1/2 cup	Dried figs
1/2 cup	Prunes
1/2 cup	Raisins
1 cup	Walnuts, crushed
1/2 cup	Sunflower seeds
3 tablespoons	Lemon juice
1 cup	Coconut

Combine the dates, figs, prunes and raisins in a food processor and finely grind them. Mix the ground fruit with the nuts and seeds. Stir in the lemon juice and shape the mixture into 1/2" balls.

Roll the balls in the coconut put them on your dehydrator trays. Dry 4-6 hours, or until crisp on the outside.

Makes about 30 balls.

Energy Bars (Version 1)

1 1/3 cup	Carob chips
1 cup	Slivered almonds
4 cups	Dried fruit
3/4 cup	Unsweetened pineapple juice
1/2 teaspoon	Almond extract
1/2 cup	Honey wheat germ

Combine 1/3 cup of the carob chips, the almonds and dried fruit in a food processor and finely grind them. In a bowl, mix the juice, extract, wheat germ and the remaining cup of carob chips.

Combine both mixtures and mix well. More juice can be added if necessary to get the mixture to stick together.

Pour onto solid fruit roll sheets on your dehydrator trays and dry for approximately 14 hours.

When nearly dry, remove the mixture from the solid trays and cut it into small squares. Put the squares back in the dehydrator, this time directly on the trays to finish drying.

Makes 24 squares.

Notes: The following fruits make good choices for this recipe: apple, raisin, date, pear, peach, apricot and pineapple.

You can coat the squares with melted chocolate, yogurt, or carob to make candy bars if desired.

Energy Bars (Version 2)

1 cup	Barley, soaked for 3 days
2 cups	Soft wheat (sprouted 1 day)
3/4 cup	Dates
3 tablespoons	Raw Honey
1 teaspoon	Cinnamon
1 teaspoon	Vanilla
1 cup	Walnuts, soaked and chopped
1/2 cup	Almonds, soaked and chopped

Combine the barley, wheat and dates in a food processor and purée. Add the honey, cinnamon, vanilla, walnuts and almonds and mix well. Form the mixture into 1/4" bars and place onto a solid fruit roll sheet on your dehydrator trays.

Dry for 6-8 hours. Half way through, remove the bars from the fruit rolls sheets, turn them over and place them directly on the trays.

Filled Fruit Appetizers

24 pieces	Dried fruit halves
3 ounces	Cream cheese, softened
3 tablespoons	Sour cream or plain yogurt
1/8 teaspoon	Paprika
1/3 cup	Monterey Jack cheese, shredded
1/3 cup	Sharp cheddar cheese, shredded
1/4 cup	Slivered almonds, chopped

Use dried fruit that is soft and pliable. If it's too hard, soak it in boiling water for 5 minutes to soften and then drain it.

In small bowl, beat the cream cheese until fluffy. Stir in the sour cream, paprika, cheese and almonds. Spoon 1 teaspoon of the mixture into the center of each piece of dried fruit.

Garnish with parsley if desired. Makes 24 appetizers.

Note: Apricots, peaches, pears and prunes work well in this recipe.

Fruit Carob Bar

3/4 cup	Dried apples
3/4 cup	Raisins
3/4 cup	Dried pears
3/4 cup	Dried peaches
1/2 cup	Dried dates
1/2 cup	Dried pineapple
1 cup	Almonds
1 1/3 cups	Carob chips
3/4 cup	Pineapple juice
1/2 cup	Wheat germ
1/2 teaspoon	Almond extract

Combine the dried fruits, almonds and 1/3 cup of carob chips in a food processor and grind.

In a bowl, combine the remaining carob chips, the pineapple juice, wheat germ and extract and mix well. Stir in the fruit mixture. If too dry, add more juice.

Form the mixture into bars and place them on solid fruit roll sheets on your dehydrator trays. If the mixture is too dry to form into bars, add more juice.

Dry for 2 1/2 hours or until firm. Remove the bars from the fruit rolls sheets, cut them into 2" pieces and place them directly on the trays. Dry for another 2 1/2 hours.

Makes approximately 30 bars.

Fruit Compote

Your choice of dried Apples, Bananas, Apricots, Pineapple, Peaches, Plums, Nectarines, Rhubarb, Strawberries, Mangos, Kiwi.

Combine as much of the dried fruits of your choice as you want. Put the fruit in a bowl and add enough water to cover it. Soak the fruit overnight or for several hours until soft.

You can add honey or sugar, grated dried lemon or orange peel and a few sticks of clove, if desired.

Honey Banana Chips

	Bananas, sliced
1/4 cup	Honey
1/4 cup	Water

Combine the honey and water to create a glaze. Dip the banana slices into the glaze and allow them to drain a little. Put them on your dehydrator trays and dry until desired consistency.

Kale Chips

Kale Chips are an excellent way to get the nutritional value of greens in your diet. Even the kids will love these!

To make Kale Chips start with 1 bunch of kale. You can experiment with different kinds of kale to find the one that you prefer. And you can also use Swiss Chard if you'd rather or are like me and have it growing abundantly in your garden.

Carefully wash the kale and remove the center stems. Tear the leaves into small pieces.

In a small bowl combine the seasoning ingredients and mix well. Pour the mixture over the kale pieces and mix to coat evenly. Place on your dehydrator trays and dry for 2-4 hours or until crispy.

Seasoning Version 1
1 tablespoon	Olive oil
1 tablespoon	Apple cider vinegar
1 teaspoon	Sea salt
1/8 cup	Parmesan cheese

Seasoning Version 2
3 tablespoons	Olive Oil
2 cloves	Garlic
1 teaspoon	Thyme

Seasoning Version 3
1 tablespoon	Olive oil
1 tablespoon	Tahini
3/4 teaspoon	Balsamic vinegar
1 teaspoon	Garlic, grated
Dash	Red peppers, crushed
	Salt and pepper to taste

Seasoning Version 4

1/2 cup	Raw sunflower seeds
1/8 cup	Sugar
1/2 tablespoon	Cinnamon
1/3 cup	Water

For this one, put the sunflower seeds, sugar and cinnamon in a food processor or blender and process, adding the water a little at a time until you get a smooth mixture. Pour the mixture over the kale pieces and dehydrate until crisp.

Seasoning Version 5

1 cup	Cashews
2 cloves	Garlic
1	Red pepper
1/4 cup	Nutritional yeast
1/4 teaspoon	Cayenne
	Salt and pepper to taste

Cover the cashews in water and let them sit for 2 hours or until soft. Drain all of the water except 1/4 cup and put them and the water in a food processor with the other ingredients except the salt and pepper. Process until smooth.

Pour the mixture over the kale pieces and place on your dehydrator trays. Sprinkle with salt and pepper to taste and dehydrate until crisp.

Muesli Bars

1/4 cup	Brown sugar
1/2 cup	Peanut butter
3 tablespoons	Butter
1/4 cup	Water
2 cups	Muesli (store bought or from the recipe on page 25)

Combine brown sugar, peanut butter and butter in a saucepan. Heat until melted then add the water and mix well. Remove from the heat and add the muesli mixing well.

Press the mixture into a loaf pan. Cool it in the refrigerator for 2 hours. Remove it from the pan and slice into bars.

Dry 8-10 hours directly on your dehydrator trays until chewy.

Oat and Nuts

4 cups	Rolled oats
1 cup	Brown sugar
1 cup	Dry roasted nuts
1 cup	Dates or apricots, chopped
1/2 cup	Raisins
1 1/2 cups	Coconut flakes

Combine all of the ingredients and mix well. Spread the mixture onto solid fruit roll sheets on your dehydrator trays.

Dry until crisp. Store in individual serving sizes in sandwich bags. They make a great snack on hikes and camping trips.

Peanut Butter and Fruit Spread

1 cup	Crunchy peanut butter
2 tablespoons	Butter, softened
1/2 cup	Dried fruit, finely chopped
1 tablespoon	Lemon juice
2 tablespoons	Honey

In a small bowl, combine all of the ingredients and beat until smooth and well mixed.

Serve on crackers, bread or celery sticks.

Note: Apples, apricots and dates are good in this recipe.

Peanut Butter Balls

2 cups	Coconut
2 cups	Dried apple slices
2/3 cup	Peanut butter
1 1/2 tablespoons	Vanilla

In a large bowl, combine all of the ingredients and mix well. Shape the mixture into 1/2" balls and put them on your dehydrator trays.

Dry 4-5 hours or until firm and crisp on the outside.

Makes 3 dozen.

Peanut Butter Patties

1/2 cup	Quick cooking oatmeal
1/2 cup	Wheat germ
1/2 cup	Coconut, shredded, toasted
1/2 cup	Slivered almonds, chopped, toasted
1/4 cup	Peanut butter
1/4 cup	Honey
1 teaspoon	Vanilla

Combine the oatmeal, wheat germ, coconut and almonds in a large bowl. Mix well. In another bowl, combine the peanut butter, honey and vanilla. Stir the peanut butter mixture into the oatmeal mixture and mix well.

Form the mixture into 1/4" thick patties and put them on lightly oiled fruit roll sheets on your dehydrator trays. Dry for 4-6 hours, or until firm and crisp. Store them in an air-tight container.

Note: You can drizzle some melted carob or chocolate on top of each patty before or after drying if desired.

Soy Sauce Cashews

1 (12 oz.) can	Dry roasted whole cashews
1/3 cup	Soy sauce
1/4 cup	Water
2 tablespoons	Garlic powder
1/4 teaspoon	Ground ginger

Put the cashews in a 9" square pan or dish. Combine the rest of the ingredients in a bowl and mix well. Pour the mixture over the nuts and let it sit overnight at room temperature.

Drain the liquid from the nuts and put them on mesh screens on your dehydrator trays. Dry for 3-5 hours or until crunchy. Store in an air-tight container.

Sunflower Wheat Crackers

1 cup	Salted sunflower seeds, roasted
1/2 cup	Butter or margarine, softened
1 cup	Whole wheat flour
1/2 cup	Bran cereal
2 tablespoons	Honey
2 tablespoons	Warm water

Grind the sunflower seeds in a food processor or blender. Put the ground sunflower seeds and the butter in a medium bowl and cream until smooth.

Add the flour, cereal, honey and water and mix well. Form the dough into a ball and put it on a large sheet of waxed paper. Shape the dough into a log. Wrap the waxed paper tightly around the dough and chill it 4-6 hours or overnight.

With a sharp knife, slice the dough into 1/4" rounds. Put them on solid fruit roll sheets on your dehydrator trays. Dry for 4-6 hours or until firm and crisp. Store in an air-tight container.

Makes approximately 50 crackers.

Sweet Potato Chips

Sweet potatoes
Olive oil
Sea salt

Cut the sweet potatoes into very thin, uniform slices. Put them in a bowl and drizzle with the olive oil. Sprinkle the sea salt on top and mix until the slices are evenly coated. Put the slices on your dehydrator trays and Dry to the desired consistency.

Variation: For a sweeter version, substitute cinnamon and brown sugar for the sea salt.

Taco Chips

1 (7 oz.) can	Whole kernel corn, drained
1 cup	Sharp cheddar cheese, grated
1/2 cup	Tomatoes, diced
1 tablespoon	Onion, chopped
1/4 teaspoon	Salt
1/8 teaspoon	Cayenne pepper
Dash	Garlic powder

Combine all of the ingredients in a blender or food processor and blend well. Spread the mixture thinly on solid fruit roll sheets on your dehydrator trays. Dry for 6-8 hours, or until dry on one side.

Remove the ring off the fruit roll sheet, turn it over and dry for 1-2 hours more, or until crisp. Break into chips.

Trail Mix (Version 1)

6 cups	Corn or other cereal flakes
1 cup	Raisins or chopped nuts
1 cup	Brown sugar
1/2 cup	Margarine, melted
1 cup	Dry roasted nuts
1 (6 oz.) package	Butterscotch chips

Combine all of the ingredients except the butterscotch chips and mix well. Spread the mixture on solid fruit roll sheets on your dehydrator trays.

Dry until crisp and let cool. Mix in the butterscotch chips and seal the mixture in small plastic bags for handy snacks.

Trail Mix (Version 2)

5 cups	Instant oatmeal
1/2 cup	Wheat germ
3/4 cup	Dried apples, chopped
3/4 cup	Raisins
1/2 cup	Dates, chopped
1 cup	Nuts, chopped
1 1/2 cups	Honey
1/2 cup	Brown sugar
1 teaspoon	Vanilla
1 teaspoon	Cinnamon

Combine all of the ingredients and mix well. Spread the mixture on solid fruit roll sheets on your dehydrator trays.

Dry until crisp. Seal in small plastic bags for handy snacks.

Trail Mix (Version 3)

1 cup	Brown sugar
1 cup	Nuts
4 cups	Rolled oats
1 teaspoon	Cinnamon
1 cup	Dates, chopped
3/4 cup	Raisins
1 cup	Coconut flakes

Combine all of the ingredients and mix well. Spread the mixture on solid fruit roll sheets on your dehydrator trays.

Dry until crisp. Seal in small plastic bags for handy snacks.

Yogurt Drops

Yogurt, any flavor

Drop the yogurt by teaspoons on lightly oiled solid fruit roll sheets on your dehydrator trays.

Dry 8-16 hours. Remove the drops from the sheets while warm and let cool. Store in refrigerator or freezer.

Notes: For variety you can sprinkle the drops with chopped peanuts or coconut before drying.

Thicker brands of yogurt generally dry better.

Zucchini Chips

Zucchini, sliced
Sesame seeds
Garlic salt

Put the zucchini slices on your dehydrator trays and lightly sprinkle them with the sesame seeds and salt.

Dry until crisp.

You can serve them as is or with a dip or ranch dressing.

Zucchini and Pineapple Chips

4 cups	Zucchini, peeled and sliced
12 ounces	Pineapple juice
3/4 cup	Sugar
1/4	Fresh lemon, juice only

In a saucepan, combine the pineapple juice, sugar and lemon juice and bring to full boil on high heat stirring frequently. Reduce heat to medium high and add the zucchini. Boil lightly for 10-15 minutes or until the slices turn a light green color. Remove them from the heat, drain, and allow them to cool.

Put the slices on your dehydrator trays. Dry for 3-5 hours or until crisp.

Note: To get a stronger flavor, let the cooked zucchini marinate in the juice for a few days. The chips will taste like sweet, zucchini pickles. If you are using small zucchinis, you can leave the soft peel on.

Desserts

Apple Cobbler

Apple Pie (Version 2) filling

1/2 cup	Dark raisins (optional)
2/3 cup	Granola
2 tablespoon	Brown sugar
2 tablespoon	Butter, softened

Preheat your oven to 350°F.

Prepare the pie filling following the **Apple Pie (Version 2)** recipe on page 93, adding the raisins if desired.

Pour the filling into a baking dish that is at least one inch deeper than the level of the filling.

Combine the granola, brown sugar and butter and mix until crumbly. Spread the topping over the filling.

Bake for 45 minutes or until the apples are tender.

Apple Cookies (Version 1)

3 cups	Red apples, cored and finely chopped
1 cup	Quick cooking oatmeal
1/4 cup	Wheat germ
1 tablespoon	Cinnamon
1 cup	Plain yogurt
1/2 cup	Unsweetened applesauce
1 tablespoon	Honey (optional)

Combine the apples, oatmeal, wheat germ and cinnamon. In a separate bowl, combine the yogurt, applesauce and honey. Pour the yogurt mixture over apple mixture and mix well.

Drop the dough by tablespoon onto solid fruit roll sheets on your dehydrator trays. Dry for 5 hours or until the cookies come off the sheets easily.

Turn them over and dry for one more hour.

Apple Cookies (Version 2)

1 cup	Dried apples, chopped
2 tablespoons	Hot water
3/4 cup	Butter
1 cup	Light brown sugar
1	Egg
2 tablespoons	Water
1 teaspoon	Vanilla
1 cup	All purpose flour
1 teaspoon	Salt
1/2 teaspoon	Baking soda
3 cups	Granola
2/3 cup	Raisins

Preheat your oven to 350° F.

Combine the dried apples and hot water and set aside.

Combine the butter, brown sugar, egg, water and vanilla and beat until creamy.

In a separate bowl, combine the flour, salt and baking soda. Add to butter mixture and mix well.

Stir in the apples without draining them, the granola and raisins. Drop the dough by teaspoonfuls onto greased baking sheets.

Bake for 15-18 minutes until lightly browned.
Makes 5 dozen.

Apple Pie (Version 1)

2 cups	Dried apples
1 cup	Sugar, brown or white
1/4 teaspoon	Salt
2 tablespoons	Flour
1	Double pie crust, prepared or homemade
1 tablespoon	Butter
1 teaspoon	Cinnamon
1/4 teaspoon	Allspice
1 tablespoon	Butter
1/4 teaspoon	Mace

Preheat your oven to 450° F.

Place the dried apples in a bowl, cover them with water and let them sit for about four hours.

Combine the sugar, salt and flour and mix in the drained, rehydrated apples. Line a pie pan with one half of the pie crust and fill with the apple mixture. Dot the top with the butter and cover with the other half of the crust.

Bake in for 15 minutes. Reduce the oven temperature to 350° F and bake for 45 minutes longer.

Variation: For a crumb crust in place of the top crust

1/2 cup	Butter or margarine
1/2 cup	Brown sugar
1/2 cup	Flour

Combine all of the ingredients and mix with a fork until crumbly. Spread evening on top of the apple mixture.

Bake in a preheated 425° oven for 15 minutes. Reduce the heat to 350° and bake for 35 minutes or until slightly browned and bubbly.

Apple Pie (Version 2)

5 cups	Dried apples slices
3 cups	Boiling water
1/2 cup	Sugar
2 tablespoon	Cornstarch
1/2 teaspoon	Cinnamon
Dash	Nutmeg
	Double pie crust, prepared or homemade
	Sugar and cinnamon

Preheat your oven to 425° F.

Combine apples and boiling water and let them stand for 15 minutes. Drain the liquid into a saucepan. Combine the sugar and cornstarch and stir into the saucepan. Add the cinnamon and nutmeg.

Cook over medium heat, stirring constantly, until the mixture boils. Add the apples and heat. Pour the apple mixture into a pastry lined pie plate. Top with remaining pastry and seal the edges.

Bake for 45 minutes or until the apples are tender.

Apple Squares

5-6 cups	Dried apples
2 cups	Boiling water
2 1/2 cups	Cake or pastry flour
1 teaspoon	Salt
1 cup + 2 tablespoons	Margarine or butter
1	Egg yolk
	Milk
1 cup	Bran flakes, crushed
2/3 cup	Sugar
1/2 teaspoon	Ground ginger
1/2 teaspoon	Cinnamon
1	Egg white, stiffly beaten
1 cup	Powdered sugar
1/2 teaspoon	Vanilla

Preheat your oven to 400°F.

Put the dried apples in a large bowl and cover them with the boiling water. Set them aside while you make the pastry.

In large bowl combine the flour and salt. Cut in the butter until crumbly. In a measuring cup lightly beat the egg yolk with a fork. Beat in enough milk to make 2/3 cup. Stir the egg mixture into the flour mixture and mix with a fork until the dough holds together. Divide the dough into two parts and roll one half on a heavily floured surface. Line a 10" x 15" jelly roll pan with the dough, pressing lightly to form the bottom crust. Sprinkle the bottom crust with the crushed bran flakes.

Drain the rehydrated apples and add the sugar, ginger, and cinnamon mixing well. Spread the apple mixture over the bottom crust. Roll out remaining dough and place it on top. Pinch the edges of the dough together to seal. Beat the egg white until stiff and brush it over top crust.

Bake 50-60 minutes or until golden brown.

Combine the powdered sugar and vanilla with enough water to make a smooth frosting.

Let pastry cool slightly, then frost while the crust is still warm. Cut into squares. Makes 15 three inch squares.

Apple Turnover

1/2	**Apple Pie (Version 2)** filling
6	Frozen pastry shells, thawed
1	Egg, lightly beaten
	Sugar, white or brown

Preheat your oven to 450° F.

Prepare one half of the pie filling following the **Apple Pie (Version 2)** recipe on page 93.

Roll out the thawed pastry shells, one at a time, on a lightly floured board, to about a 7-inch square. Spoon the filling onto center of each pastry square.

Brush the edges with the egg and fold over one half of the square to form a triangle. Seal the edges with fork. Brush the tops with more beaten egg to glaze and sprinkle with sugar. Cut 2 air vents in each triangle.

Put the turnovers on an ungreased baking sheet and bake for 20 minutes or until browned.

Banana Nut Cookies

Make the **Apple Cookies (Version 2)** recipe on page 91 with the following adjustments:
    Substitute 1 cup chopped dried bananas for the apples
    Increase the flour to 1 1/2 cups
    Omit raisins and granola
    Add 1 cup uncooked regular oatmeal
    Add 1 cup chopped nuts

Carrot Cookies

1 cup	Dried grated carrots
1/2 cup	Hot water
3/4 cup	Butter or margarine
1 cup	Light brown sugar
1	Egg
2 tablespoons	Water
1 teaspoon	Vanilla
2 cups	All purpose flour
1 teaspoon	Salt
1/2 teaspoon	Baking soda
1/2 teaspoon	Cinnamon
1/4 teaspoon	Nutmeg
1 (6 oz.) package	Chocolate chips (optional)

Preheat your oven to 350° F and lightly grease baking sheets.

Combine the dried carrots and hot water and set aside for 30 minutes, stirring twice.

Combine the butter or margarine, brown sugar, egg, water, and vanilla and beat until creamy.

Combine the flour, salt, baking soda, cinnamon, and nutmeg and mix well. Add the flour mixture to the butter mixture and mix well. Fold in the drained carrots and chocolate chips if desired.

Drop the dough by teaspoonfuls onto the baking sheets.

Bake for 15-18 minutes or until lightly browned.
Makes 4 dozen.

Carrot Cake (Version 1)

1 cup	Dried carrots
1 cup	Warm water
1 1/2 cups	Vegetable oil
3	Eggs
1 1/2 cups	Sugar
2 cups	Whole wheat flour
2 teaspoons	Baking soda
1/2 teaspoon	Salt
2 1/2 teaspoon	Cinnamon
Dash	Nutmeg
1 cup	Walnuts, chopped
1 cup	Crushed pineapple, drained

Put the dried carrots and warm water in a bowl and set aside for 30 minutes to rehydrate the carrots. Do not drain.

Preheat your oven to 350° F and grease and flour a 10" tube, Bundt or springform pan.

Combine the oil, eggs and sugar and beat until well mixed. Add the remaining ingredients including the carrots without draining them and mix well. Pour into the prepared pan. Bake for one hour. Cool for 5-10 minutes in pan and then remove. Cool completely and frost with cream cheese icing.

Note: You can substitute 3/4 cup oil and 3/4 cup applesauce for the 1 1/2 cups of oil.

Cream Cheese Icing

2 (8 oz.) packages	Cream cheese, softened
1 cup	Powdered sugar
1 teaspoon	Vanilla
3/4 cup	Coconut, shredded

Combine the ingredients and mix well with a beater. Frost the cooled cake with the icing and sprinkle the coconut on top.

Carrot Cake (Version 2)

2 cups	Dried grated carrot
2 cups	Boiling water
1 cup	Sugar
1 cup	Vegetable oil
2 cups	All purpose flour
1 teaspoon	Baking powder
Pinch	Salt
2 teaspoons	Cinnamon
4	Eggs
1/2 cup	Walnuts, chopped

Preheat your oven to 350° F and grease a cake baking dish.

Combine carrots and boiling water in a bowl and let stand for one hour to rehydrate. Drain.

Combine the carrots, sugar and oil and mix well. Add the dry ingredients, eggs and nuts and mix again.

Pour the batter into the baking dish and bake 30-35 minutes until done.

Fruit Filled Cookies

1/2 cup	Butter or margarine
1/2 cup	Brown sugar
1/2 cup	Granulated sugar
1	Egg
1 teaspoon	Vanilla extract
2 cups	All purpose flour
1/4 teaspoon	Baking soda
1/4 teaspoon	Salt

Prepare dried fruit filling following the recipe on the next page and let it cool before using.

Combine the butter or margarine with sugars and beat until creamed. Add the egg and vanilla and beat well.

In another bowl, combine the flour, baking soda and salt. Add the dry mixture to the butter mixture and mix well. Divide the dough in half.

Flour a large sheet of waxed paper. Roll out each half of dough to a 12"x9" rectangle. Spread the dough with the filling. Starting with the long side, roll it up tightly to make a 12 inch long roll. Wrap the roll in the waxed paper and refrigerate for 4 hours.

Preheat oven to 375°F and grease cookie sheets.

Cut the chilled rolls into 1/4 inch slices. Bake the cookies for 6-8 minutes until the edges are golden. Makes about 80 cookies.

Fruit Filling

1 1/2 cups	Dried figs, dates and raisins, pineapple, apricots, and/or prunes, finely chopped
1/2 cup	Water
1/2 cup	Sugar (optional)
1 teaspoon	Lemon juice
1/2 teaspoon	Grated lemon peel
1/3 cup	Nuts, chopped

In a saucepan, combine the dried fruit, water, and sugar. Cook the mixture over a low heat 20-25 minutes until thickened, stirring frequently. When thickened, add the lemon juice, lemon peel and nuts. Cool.

Note: For extra flavor you can substitute orange or pineapple juice for the water.

Oatmeal Cookies

1 cup	Butter or margarine
1 cup	Brown sugar
1/2 cup	Granulated sugar
2	Eggs
1 1/2 teaspoons	Vanilla
2 cups	All purpose flour
1 teaspoon	Baking powder
1 teaspoon	Baking soda
1/2 teaspoon	Salt
1-1/2 cups	Dried apricots, peaches, pears, pineapple, or cherries, chopped
2 1/2 cups	Old fashioned oats

Preheat oven to 350°F.

Combine the butter or margarine and sugars and beat until creamed. Add the eggs and vanilla and mix well.

In another bowl, combine the dry ingredients except the oats. In a food processor or blender, process the oats until fine and add to the dry mixture. Stir in the dried fruit.

Combine the dry and butter mixtures and mix well. Shape the dough into small balls. Flatten on a cookie sheet.

Bake 7-8 minutes or until the edges are golden brown.
Makes 3 dozen cookies.

Peach Pie

1 1/2 cups	Dried peaches
2 tablespoons	Water
1 1/2 tablespoons	Cinnamon
1/2 cup	White or brown sugar
2 tablespoons	Flour
4 tablespoons	Butter, melted
1/8 teaspoon	Salt
2	Prepared pie crusts

Put the dried peaches in a bowl with the water and refrigerate overnight.

Preheat oven to 350°F.

Cook the peaches over low heat about 45 minutes until soft. When soft, chop the peaches.

Combine the rest of the ingredients in a bowl and mix well. Stir in the peaches. Pour the mixture into a pie pan lined with one of the pie crusts, cover with the other crust.

Bake 35-45 minutes until golden brown.

Pineapple Coconut Cookies

Make the **Apple Cookies (Version 2)** recipe on page 91 with the following adjustments:

    Substitute 1 cup chopped dried pineapple for the apples.

    Decrease the granola to 2 cups.

    Add 1 cup flaked coconut.

    Omit the raisins.

Strawberry Yogurt Ice Cream

1 cup	Plain or flavored yogurt
1/2 cup	Dried strawberries
2 tablespoons	Sugar

Combine the strawberries and sugar and mix well. Add the mixture to the yogurt and freeze it until it thickens. Remove from the freezer and stir. Return to the freezer until solid. Makes two servings.

Notes: You can substitute almost any dried fruit or combination of fruits for this recipe.

You can double or triple this recipe and freeze it in your ice cream maker.

This is the recipe pictured at the beginning of this section made in my ice cream maker.

For Your Pets

~Dogs~

Beef Strips

1 pound	Flank steak
2 cups	Water
1 teaspoon	Ground sage
1 tablespoon	Beef bouillon, dry

Put the steak and water in a large frying pan and cook over a low heat. Sprinkle the meat with the sage and beef bouillon.

Let the meat simmer until it is thoroughly cooked. Remove the meat, letting it drain and cut into long strips. Kitchen scissors do this well.

Put the strips on your dehydrator trays and dry for 3-5 hours or until completely dry. Store in a baggie in the refrigerator.
Notes: These treats can also be frozen.

You can use stew beef or roast trimming if desired to make small pieces of meat instead of strips.

Be sure the bouillon you use has no added ingredients, especially no onion or garlic which can be harmful to dogs. If you want, you can omit the bouillon and/or the sage.

Dehydrated Dog Food

Frozen, raw dog food, thawed
or
Canned dog food

This is a very simple idea for picky eaters like my dog! She doesn't like to eat frozen raw if it's very soft and wet so I came up with this idea and it was a hit.

Start with the frozen raw or canned dog food of your choice from your local store. Form it into small patties, squeezing out any extra liquid so it will dry quicker.

Dry for about 4 hours until you reach the consistency your dog likes. It can be chewy like jerky or crisp.

Store in a baggie or closed bowl in the refrigerator.

This is what is pictured at the start of this section. Dinner is served!

Jerky Sticks

1 pound	Ground beef
1/2 cup	Canned red kidney beans
1 cup	Zucchini, fresh, chopped
1/2 cup	Applesauce
1/2 teaspoon	Ground sage

In a skillet, cook the ground beef until completely cooked throughout. Break up any chunks so it is crumbled when done.

Drain the liquid from kidney beans and set aside. Put the beans and zucchini in food processor or blender and process until you get a smooth, thick paste.

Add the meat, applesauce and sage and process again. If the mixture is too thick, add a little of the reserved liquid from beans. The mixture is done when there are no chunks of meat or beans and it is not too wet.

Put the round tip on your jerky maker gun and fill it with the mixture. Press out four inch long treats directly on your dehydrator trays.

Dry 3-5 hours until completely dry.

Store in a baggie in the refrigerator.

Pumpkin

2	Eggs
1 cup	Water
1/2 cup	Oil
1 cup	Canned pumpkin
2 cups	Whole wheat flour
1/2 cup	Cornmeal
1/2 cup	Oats
2 teaspoons	Cinnamon

Combine the eggs, water, oil and pumpkin and mix well.

In another bowl, combine the dry ingredients and mix well.

Add the dry mixture to the wet and form into a ball. Place the ball of dough onto a floured board and roll out to about 1/4 inch thick. Shape the dough into bars, squares or cut out with a small cookie cutter.

Dry 6-8 hours or until very dry and crisp.

Note: Be sure to used plain canned pumpkin, not pie filling.

Turkey and Sweet Potato

2 cups	Cooked turkey
1 cup	Water
1 cup	Sweet potato, cooked until soft
1 tablespoon	Molasses
1 1/2 cups	Old fashioned oatmeal (not cooked)
3 dozen	Cranberries, fresh or frozen (optional)

Cut the turkey into small pieces and put it with the water in a food processor or blender. Process until it is a smooth, thick paste consistency with no meat chunks.

Add the sweet potato and molasses and process again.

Pour the mixture into a large bowl and add the oatmeal. Mix well to form a soft dough. If it is too wet, add a little more oatmeal.

Spoon the dough onto your dehydrator trays and if desired, put a cranberry on top of each one, pressing slightly so it will stay.

Dehydrate 4-5 hours or until completely dry but not crispy. Store in a baggie in the refrigerator.

Note: You can substitute blueberries for the cranberries and white potatoes for the sweet potatoes if desired.

My next recipe book will be all sorts of treats for your dog. Look for it coming very soon!

Catnip Shrimp

1 (4 oz.) can   Small peeled shrimp, drained
1/3 cup   Catnip flowers, fresh

Chop the catnip flowers into small pieces discarding the stems.

Combine the catnip and shrimp and mix well being careful to keep the shrimp whole.

Put the shrimp and flowers onto your dehydrator trays.

Dry for about two hours or until completely dry.

Store in a baggie or closed bowl in the refrigerator.

Notes: If you can't find fresh catnip flowers in your local store, you can grow your own or use dried catnip. To use dried catnip, dry the shrimp alone and then add the dried catnip when you give it to your cat.

If you want to grow your own, you can get catnip plants at your local nursery in the herb section. It grows well in a sunny spot in the ground or in a pot. In a couple of months the plant should blossom so you can pick some of the flowers for this recipe.

If you get an abundance of flowers, you can dry them separately for 2-3 hours.

Salmon Cookies

1 (6 oz.) can	Salmon, packed in water, undrained
1/3 cup	Water (if needed)
2 cups	Oat bran flour

Put the salmon, including the water in the can, in a food processor or blender and process until it is a smooth, thick paste. If the mixture is too thick, add a small amount of water, but don't let the mixture get too soupy.

Spoon the paste into a bowl and add the flour, mixing well to make a thick dough. If it's too wet, add a little bit more flour until you can form a ball.

Place the ball of dough onto a floured board and roll out to about 1/4 inch thick. Cut the dough with a small cookie cutter and place them on your dehydrator racks. With a sharp knife, score each cookie crosswise so that when done, the cookie can be broken into four pieces.

Dry for 4-5 hours or until crisp and crunchy.

Store in a baggie or closed bowl in the refrigerator.

Salmon Grass

| 1 (6 oz.) can | Salmon, packed in water, drained |
| 1/3 cup | Cat grass, fresh |

Chop the salmon and cat grass into small pieces and combine in a bowl. Mix well.

Put the mixture on mesh screens on your dehydrator trays. Some of the grass will stick to the fish but not all. It will still dehydrate well.

Dry for 2-3 hours or until the salmon pieces are completely dry. Store the fish and grass in a baggie or closed bowl in the refrigerator.

Notes: The cat grass used in this recipe is oat, wheat or barley grass grown inside specifically for your cat. If you've never grown grass for your cat before, you can start with a kit like the Rocket Cats Garden Kit.

Or you can substitute catnip for the cat grass. You can also substitute canned tuna for the salmon.

Tuna Crackers

2 (6 oz.) cans	Tuna, packed in water, undrained
1 cup	Cornmeal
1 1/3 cups	Flour
1/2 cup	Water

Combine all of the ingredients and mix well.

Roll the dough on a floured board to 1/4 inch thickness and cut it into small shapes with a cookie cutter.

Dry for 2-3 hours or until crisp and crunchy. Store in a baggie or closed bowl in the refrigerator.

~Birds~

Honey Brittle

2 1/4 cups	Grape Nuts or Cheerios, crushed
2 1/4 cups	Bird food pellets, crushed
2 cups	Mixed bird seeds
1 1/2 cups	Honey

Combine the dry ingredients and mix well. Stir in the honey a little at a time until the mixture is moist but not wet.

Spread the mixture on fruit roll sheets on your dehydrator trays. Dry for 1 1/2-2 1/2 hours or until brittle.

Store in a baggie or closed bowl in the refrigerator.

Note: You should use a cereal as low in zinc as possible. Zinc in high doses can harm your bird, so keep the amount in the cereal low and don't give your bird too many at a time.

Applesauce Cookies

2 1/2 cups	Applesauce
2 1/2 cups	Mixed birdseed
1 cup	Frozen mixed vegetables

Combine the ingredients and mix well. Coat the inside of a few cookie cutters with spray vegetable oil. Put the cookie cutters on an oiled fruit roll sheet on your dehydrator trays. Fill the cookie cutters with the mixture, packing tightly.

Dry the cookies until the cookie cutter can be removed. Turn them over and dry some more until they are hard on both sides.

Note: You can hang them in your bird's cage by pushing a needle and heavy thread through one side.

~Horses~

Peppermint Apple

2 1/4 cups	Flour
1 cup	Oats
1/3 cup	Molasses
1 cup	Applesauce
	Water
12	Peppermint candies, crushed
1 medium	Apple

Combine the flour and oats and mix well. Stir in the molasses. Slowly stir in the applesauce and enough water to form a soft but not wet dough. Stir in the peppermints and apple.

Dry for 10-12 hours or until completely dry.

Sunflower Apple

1/3 cup	Sunflower seeds
2 1/4 cups	Flour
2/3 cup	Apples, chopped
1/4 cup	Carrots, peas, or other vegetables
1/4 cup	Oats, ground to powder
1 1/4 cup	Peanut butter
1 cup	Rolled oats
1 cup	Molasses

Combine the ingredients and mix well. Add enough molasses to make a stiff dough.

Roll the dough on a floured board and cut into squares.

Dry 4 hours or until very dry.

~Bunnies and Gerbils~

1 small	Carrot, puréed
1	Banana, mashed
1 teaspoon	Honey
1/4 cup	Rabbit or gerbil pellets, finely ground
1/3 cup	Flour

Combine the carrot, banana and honey and mix well. Stir in the pellet powder and flour and mix well to form a dough.

Knead the dough for 1-2 minutes and roll out on a floured board to about 1/4" thickness.

Cut into squares or shapes with a small cookie cutter.

Dry for 10-12 hours until very dry.

Index

Recipes for Dehydrating

Recipes for Using Dehydrated Ingredients

About the Author

Cathy L. Kidd is a craftsperson at heart. For as long as she can remember she has been creating things with her hands. She has done crochet (taught to her by her Aunt Carol), stained glass (learned by taking a class), candlemaking (learned from an ebook) and cooking (learned initially from Betty Crocker!)

Her homemade recipe books specialize in recipes for your kitchen appliances, in this case your dehydrator. Her other books include:

- Homemade Bread Recipes – A Simple and Easy Bread Machine Cookbook
- Homemade Soup Recipes: Simple and Easy Slow Cooker Recipes
- How to Make Homemade Ice Cream: Simple and Easy Ice Cream Maker Recipes
- How to Make Smoothies: Simple, Easy and Healthy Blender Recipes

For more recipes visit: www.easyhomemadebreadrecipes.com and join us on Facebook at https://www.facebook.com/RecipesForYourKitchenAppliances

Lightning Source UK Ltd.
Milton Keynes UK
UKOW06f1853250316

270908UK00014B/140/P